TABLE OF CONTENTS

For the Teacher

This reproducible study guide consists of lessons to use in conjunction with the novel *The Secret Garden*. Written in chapter-by-chapter format, the guide contains a synopsis, pre-reading activities, vocabulary and comprehension exercises, as well as extension activities to be used as follow-up to the novel.

In a homogeneous classroom, whole class instruction with one title is appropriate. In a heterogeneous classroom, reading groups should be formed: each group works on a different novel at its reading level. Depending upon the length of time devoted to reading in the classroom, each novel, with its guide and accompanying lessons, may be completed in three to six weeks.

Begin using NOVEL-TIES for reading development by distributing the novel and a folder to each child. Distribute duplicated pages of the study guide for students to place in their folders. After examining the cover and glancing through the book, students can participate in several pre-reading activities. Vocabulary questions should be considered prior to reading a chapter; all other work should be done after the chapter has been read. Comprehension questions can be answered orally or in writing. The classroom teacher should determine the amount of work to be assigned, always keeping in mind that readers must be nurtured and that the ultimate goal is encouraging students' love of reading.

The benefits of using NOVEL-TIES are numerous. Students read good literature in the original, rather than in abridged or edited form. The good reading habits, formed by practice in focusing on interpretive comprehension and literary techniques, will be transferred to the books students read independently. Passive readers become active, avid readers.

SYNOPSIS

Mary Lennox, an ignored unwanted child, born in India to English parents, grows to become a lonely, self-centered, sullen ten year old. When her parents die in a cholera epidemic, Mary is sent to live with her widowed uncle who is grieving for his wife at Misselthwaite Manor in Yorkshire, England. Soon after Mary arrives, her uncle goes off on an extended trip, leaving her in the care of servants.

Mary is fascinated by the moors with their strange beauty, the one-hundred-room house with its many treasures, and the mysterious secret garden which has been shut up since the death of her aunt ten years earlier. Mary's maid, Martha, and Martha's brother, Dickon, introduce Mary to the goodness and laughter of life. Dickon loves the moors and enjoys nature, developing friendships with animals and birds. After Mary finds the secret garden with the help of a robin, Dickon helps her tend it. The garden affords Mary a genuine interest for the first time in her life.

Mary, who thought she was the only child living at Misselthwaite, discovers her bed-ridden hypochondriac cousin Colin. She helps to calm his tantrums by telling him of Dickon; later, she reveals the secret of the garden. Sensing his excitement, the friends plan to get him outside and into the garden which he has never seen. In the garden they work and plan together and learn to laugh and play. Fresh air, healthy appetite, friendship, and caring for growing plants prove to be restoratives far superior to the medicines Colin was using.

As they regain healthy bodies and spirits, Mary and Colin experience an almost magical change. They change from spoiled, self-centered children to loving, pleasant young adults.

PRE-READING ACTIVITIES

1. Preview the book by reading the title and the author's name and by looking at the illustration on the cover. Do you know anything about this book? Have you seen a film based on the book? Where and when do you think it takes place? What do you think it is about? Have you read anything else written by Frances Hodgson Burnett?

2. *The Secret Garden*, first published in 1911, is considered a classic for young readers. What qualities do you think make a book a classic? Compile a list of books that you have read that could be considered classics. What qualities do these books possess that make them both enduring and endearing to young people?

3. Go online to find photographs of Yorkshire, England that show a country manor house, a country cottage, and the moors. From a book or a website about flowers, find pictures of plants that grow wild on the moor, such as heather and gorse. Also, look at pictures of flowers that are cultivated in English country gardens, such as roses, daffodils, crocuses, and lilies-of-the-valley. Share these images with your classmates.

4. To understand the world from which Mary has come, collect pictures of British life in India under colonial rule. Domestic scenes of British families with their man servants will help you imagine Mary's background.

5. Cultivate a windowsill flower garden. Obtain a large window box, potting soil, and several varieties of seed for easy-growing flowers, such as marigolds, zinnias, and asters. Seeds must be kept warm and well watered. When the seedlings have several sets of leaves they should be pinched to encourage bush growth.

6. **Pair/Share:** Discuss with a partner what could happen to children if parents gave them money and all the things that money could buy, but offered no guidance, discipline, or care. Conclusions drawn from this discussion will lead you to a better understanding of Mary and Colin when you encounter them in the book.

7. **Cooperative Learning Activity:** Much of this book is written in Yorkshire dialect. To accustom yourself to the difficulties in reading and understanding dialect, read these passages aloud and translate them into standard English with a cooperative learning group.

8. **Art Connection:** Poets throughout the ages have written poems about flowers. You and your classmates may search through poetry anthologies to locate many of these poems. Each student should copy one poem and illustrate it with a sketch or picture from a flower catalog. Display these illustrated poems on a bulletin board and refer to them as you read the book.

9. Become familiar with these Indian terms and their meanings:

Ayah	native nurse
Dervish	member of an Islamic religious sect noted for devotional exercises
Fakirs	magicians
Hindustani	Indian dialect
Mahout	driver of elephants
Mem Sahib	mistress of the house
Missie Sahib	daughter of the mistress
Palanquin	enclosed seat for one person
Rajah	Indian prince
Salaam	bowing very low, placing right palm on forehead

CHAPTER 1

Vocabulary: Draw a line from each word on the left to its definition on the right. Then use the numbered words to fill in the blanks in the sentences below.

1. cholera
2. tyrannical
3. veranda
4. bungalow
5. desolation
6. compound

a. one-story house; cottage
b. severe, infectious, often fatal disease
c. state of being wretched and lonely
d. enclosure containing residences and businesses of Europeans in the Orient
e. unjustly cruel or harsh
f. open porch, usually roofed and attached to the side of a house

. . . .

1. The young woman had a terrible feeling of _____ as she stood alone in the empty house where she had once lived.

2. The little _____ had a cozy feeling since the bedrooms and the living area were all on the same floor.

3. As soon as the patient feels well enough, she may sit outdoors on the _____.

4. If a child is always allowed to have his own way, he might develop a _____ disposition.

5. With fears of an uprising among the people in the village, those in the _____ asked for tighter security.

6. After the _____ outbreak in southern India, all of the hospitals were full to overflowing.

> Read to find out how the cholera epidemic affected Mary's life.

Questions:

1. In what ways has Mary, a child of wealth, been neglected?
2. How did neglect affect Mary's personality?
3. What extraordinary events occurred while Mary slept?
4. Why were the men surprised to see a child in the house?

Chapter 1 (cont.)

Questions for Discussion:

1. Why do you think Mary's parents neglected their only child?

2. Do you think it is possible for a spoiled child to grow up to be an unspoiled adult?

Background Information:

The first chapter consists of background information about Mary Lennox to set the stage for all that will happen next. Fill in the chart below to tell what you have learned about Mary.

Age:_____

Country of birth: _____

Family background: _____

_____

_____

_____

_____

Appearance: _____

_____

_____

Personality: _____

_____

_____

_____

Writing Activity:

Pretend you are Mary Lennox. Write a journal entry describing the events you have seen and your feelings about them.

CHAPTERS 2, 3

Vocabulary: Synonyms are words with similar meanings. Draw a line from each word in column A to its synonym in column B. Then use the words in column A to fill in the blanks in the sentences below.

A	B
1. impudent	a. carriage
2. stout	b. shy
3. brougham	c. argue
4. timid	d. rude
5. massive	e. bulky
6. quarrel	f. fat

. . . .

1. Having received little instruction in good manners, the little girl did not even know she was being _____.

2. Long ago, wealthy travelers went from place to place by horse-driven _____, while poor people traveled by foot.

3. The two brothers decided it was better to live in peace than to _____ all the time.

4. I decided to go on a diet when I became too _____ to fit into my clothes.

5. Watching my sister lecture before a large audience made it hard for me to believe she was once too _____ to speak to strangers.

6. No matter how hard I pushed, I could not open the _____ steel door.

> Read to learn about Misselthwaite Manor, Mary's new home.

Questions:

1. Why does Mrs. Medlock tell Mary all about Misselthwaite Manor before they arrive?

2. How does Mary react to Mrs. Medlock's description of Misselthwaite Manor? Why do you think she reacts that way?

3. What makes Misselthwaite Manor seem strange and lonely?

4. What kind of welcome does Mary receive at her uncle's home?

Chapters 2, 3 (cont.)

Art Connection:

Near the end of Chapter Three, the author uses vivid words to describe Misselthwaite Manor. Reread this section of the book and either draw a picture of the Manor or find an illustration that looks like the Manor.

Science Connection: Cholera

Cholera is an infectious disease of the intestines which caused the epidemic that killed Mary's parents and so many people in India. Do some research on the disease of cholera to find out its history, cause, treatment, and whether it is still a threat. Choose three other infectious diseases and find out about them. What advances has modern science made in wiping out these diseases?

Geography/Math Connection:

Use a globe or an atlas to locate India and England. Trace the route that Mary took to get to Yorkshire.

- How many miles is it from India to London, England? How long would it take to travel by ship? By plane? How much faster is it by plane?

- How many miles is it from London to Yorkshire? How long do you think it would take to travel by horse and carriage? By automobile? How much time would you save?

- How many miles is it from your city to London? How would you travel today? How long would it take?

- When it is 9:00 A.M. in your city, what time is it in London? How many hours difference is it?

Writing Activity:

Mary has no friends and does not show her feelings. Nevertheless, imagine you are Mary and write a letter to someone you might have known in India. In this letter describe the journey, your companion Mrs. Medlock, and your arrival at Misselthwaite Manor.

CHAPTERS 4, 5

Vocabulary: Antonyms are words with opposite meanings. Draw a line from each word in column A to its antonym in column B. Then use the words in column A to fill in the blanks in the sentences below.

A	B
1. substantial	a. haughty
2. languid	b. frail
3. ceased	c. commenced
4. sturdy	d. energetic
5. servile	e. pleasant
6. surly	f. inadequate

. . . .

1. The waiter's _____ manner disguised his feelings of disdain for his customers.

2. When the room temperature climbed near ninety degrees, everyone became _____ and sleepy.

3. If you expect your luggage to be handled roughly, be sure to pack a _____ suitcase.

4. A _____ attitude will not win you any friends or customers.

5. I need to eat a _____ breakfast or I become irritable by noon.

6. We enjoyed the peace and quiet once the loud music _____.

> Read to find out how Mary comes to terms with her own loneliness.

Questions:

1. How is Martha different from other servants Mary has known?

2. Why do Martha and Mary have such different opinions of dark-skinned people?

3. What makes Mary realize that she is lonely?

4. How does Mary discover the location of the secret garden?

5. What does the author mean when she says: "The fresh wind from the moor had begun to blow the cobwebs out of her young brain and to waken her up a little?"

6. Near the end of Chapter Five, the author mentions four good things happening to Mary. What are they and why are they considered good?

Chapters 4, 5 (cont.)

Literary Devices:

I. *Cliffhanger*—A device borrowed from serialized silent movies, the cliffhanger in literature is a suspenseful end to an episode. What is the cliffhanger at the end of Chapter Five?

_____

II. *Simile*—A simile is a figure of speech in which two unlike objects are compared using the words "like" or "as." For example, when Martha talks about her brother and sisters she says:

> They're as hungry as young hawks an' foxes.

What is being compared?

_____

What is the effect of this comparison?

_____

_____

Find another simile in these chapters and tell what is being compared.

_____

_____

Literary Element: Characterization

Use a Venn diagram, such as the one below, to compare Mary and Ben Weatherstaff. Write about the qualities they have in common in the overlapping part of the circles.

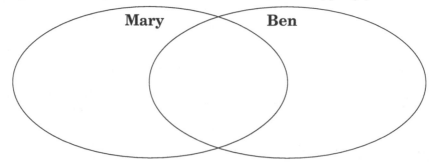

Writing Activity:

Write a dialogue that might have taken place between Martha and her mother. Have Martha tell her mother all about Mary, the strange little girl who has just come to the Manor. Do not attempt to write this in a Yorkshire dialect.

CHAPTERS 6 – 8

Vocabulary: Analogies are word equations in which the first pair of words has the same relationship as the second pair of words. For example: FORTUNATE is to LUCKY as PRETTY is to ATTRACTIVE. Both pairs of words are synonyms. Choose the best word from the Word Box to complete each of the following analogies.

```
                         WORD BOX
     coax        corridor      muffled       torrent
     collie      denial        scowl
```

1. COMPLIMENT is to SMILE as CRITICISM is to _____.

2. VISION is to BLURRED as SOUND is to _____.

3. SNOW is to BLIZZARD as RAIN is to _____.

4. PERSUADE is to _____ as ASK is to INQUIRE.

5. POLITE is to IMPUDENT as _____ is to PERMISSION.

6. CANARY is to BIRD as _____ is to DOG.

7. ROOM is to CHAMBER as HALLWAY is to _____.

> Read to find out how the robin helps Mary get her wish.

Questions:

1. How is Mary's attitude toward Martha changing?

2. Why is Mary interested in the library at Misselthwaite Manor?

3. How does Mrs. Medlock react when she finds Mary wandering through the corridors at the Manor?

4. Why can't Ben Weatherstaff answer Mary's questions about the garden?

5. How does Mary discover the door to the secret garden?

6. Why is Mary anxious to find the secret garden?

Chapters 6 – 8 (cont.)

Questions for Discussion:

1. Why do you think Mary is fond of Martha's mother and Dickon before she even meets them?

2. Why do you think Mrs. Medlock contradicts Mary's report that someone was crying?

3. What do you think Mary is learning about life by observing Martha's attitude and activities?

4. Why do you think Mary is becoming less contrary?

Literary Device: Cliffhanger

What is the cliffhanger at the end of Chapter Eight?

_____

_____

Writing Activity:

At the end of Chapter Eight Mary is about to enter the secret garden. Before you read the next chapter, write a detailed description of what you think Mary will see. In your imagination tell what she will see in every corner of the garden. If you can, give the names of specific flowers and trees. Indicate whether plants are alive or faded. Then compare your imagined description with the one at the beginning of Chapter Nine.

CHAPTERS 9, 10

Vocabulary: Draw a line from each word on the left to its definition on the right. Then use the numbered words to fill in the blanks in the sentences below.

1. tendrils
2. alcove
3. civil
4. sarcastic
5. obstinate
6. trowel
7. spade

a. stubborn
b. tool for digging, usually with a blade that is narrower and flatter than a shovel
c. gardening tool with curved blade used for taking up plants and turning up earth
d. recessed space or small room opening out of a room
e. cutting or derisive
f. threadlike vines that twine around another object
g. courteous; polite

. . . .

1. A(n) _____ is a good tool to use if you need to dig a deep trench around a tree.

2. I was very embarrassed when the teacher made _____ remarks about my missing homework assignment.

3. The _____ of the ivy plant wrapped around the drain pipe, causing it to clog at the top and bottom.

4. I used a(n) _____ to remove the tulip bulbs from my garden.

5. My brother is so _____ that he will not apologize even when he knows he is wrong.

6. I was left standing in the _____ before being invited into the conference room for an interview.

7. If you are _____ to the people you work with, they will cooperate and work harder.

> Read to learn about Mary and Dickon's first meeting.

Questions:

1. Why does Mary become excited when she finds "sharp, pale green points" sticking out of the earth in the secret garden?

2. What evidence shows that Mary has grown healthier in the month since her arrival at Misselthwaite?

3. Why does Mary think she must keep the garden a secret?

Chapters 9, 10 (cont.)

4. Why does Mary ask Martha if the scullery-maid had a toothache?

5. To whom is Ben referring when he tells Mary that he once gardened for a young woman who had him plant many rose bushes?

6. Why does Mary know it is Dickon before he introduces himself?

Questions for Discussion:

1. Why do you think Mary gets such pleasure out of hard physical labor in the garden?

2. Why do you think Mary trusts Dickon enough to show him the secret garden?

Yorkshire Dialect: Explain each of the following statements that were spoken in Yorkshire dialect. Also, identify the speaker.

1. Children's as good as 'rithmetic to set you findin' out things.

   _____

2. He's as full o' pride as an egg's full o' meat.

   _____

3. Tha' looked like a young plucked crow when tha' first came into this garden.

   _____

Literary Device: Personification

Personification is a literary device in which an author grants lifelike qualities to nonhuman objects. For example:

> . . . dozens and dozens of the tiny, pale green points were to be
> seen in cleared places, looking twice as cheerful as they had looked
> before when the grass and weeds had been smothering them.

What is being personified?

_____

Why do you think the author used this device?

_____

Writing Activity:

Write about a place that is special to you. Tell what about this place appeals to you most. Is it a special room, a beach, a favorite vacation spot, or a secret place where you can be alone?

CHAPTERS 11 – 13

Vocabulary: In each word group, circle the one word that does not belong. On the line below, tell how the other words are alike.

1. narcissus   crocus   evergreen   daffodil

    The other words all_____

    _____

2. melancholy   exultant   ecstatic   blissful

    The other words all_____

    _____

3. forest   swamp   moor   constellation

    The other words all_____

    _____

4. robin   otter   thrush   sparrow

    The other words all_____

    _____

5. scullery-maid   governess   nurse   landlord

    The other words all_____

    _____

> Read to learn the source of the crying sounds.

Questions:

1. How is Dickon able to assure Mary that there will be roses in the garden in the spring?

2. Mary tells Dickon he is the fifth person she likes. Who are the other four?

3. What does Dickon mean when he assures Mary that she is "safe as a missel thrush"?

4. Why is Mr. Craven willing to postpone getting Mary a governess?

5. Why do Mary and Colin each think the other is a ghost?

6. Why does Mr. Craven ignore Colin? Why does Mr. Craven insist that the servants obey all of Colin's wishes?

Chapters 11 – 13 (cont.)

7. How does Mary convince Colin that he should not have the servants take him to the secret garden?

8. What are the first gestures of affection that Mary has ever offered?

Questions for Discussion:

1. What do you think Colin finds so strange about Mary? Why does he like her?

2. Why do you think Mr. Craven is willing to give Mary "a bit of earth"?

3. How do you think Mary and Colin will be able to help each other?

Science Connection:

Make a list of all the plants that Mary and Dickon find in the secret garden. Locate pictures of these plants and do some research to learn about the care they need.

Literary Devices:

I. *Dramatic Irony*—Dramatic irony is a device wherein the reader or the audience sees a character's mistakes or misunderstandings which the character is unable to see himself or herself.

    What is ironic about Mary's request to Mr. Craven and his positive response that she be allowed to take a bit of earth from anywhere on his property?

    _____

    _____

    _____

II. *Symbolism*—A symbol in literature is an object, person, or event that represents an idea or set of ideas. What are the many things a key symbolizes at Misselthwaite Manor?

    _____

    _____

    _____

    _____

Chapters 11 – 13 (cont.)

Literary Element: Characterization

Use the Venn diagram to compare the characters of Colin, Mary, and Dickon. Write about their similarities in the overlapping parts of the circles.

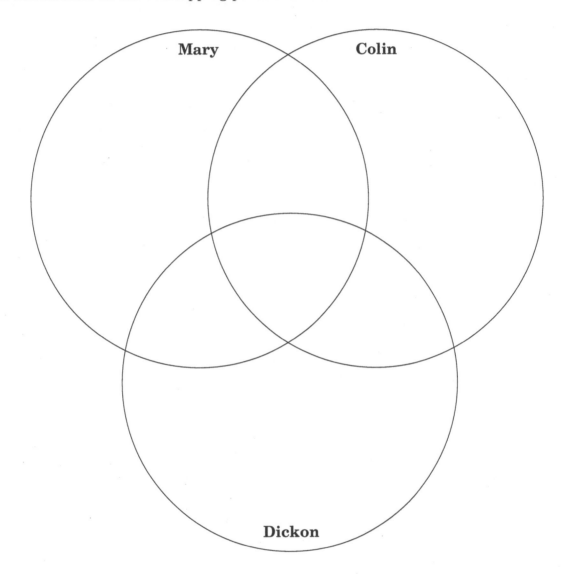

Writing Activity:

Write about an important friendship in your life. Tell what special qualities each of you offers the other.

CHAPTERS 14, 15

Vocabulary: Use the context to determine the meaning of the underlined word in each of the following sentences. Circle the letter of the answer you choose.

1. I was so proud of my brother for winning the race that I <u>boasted</u> about it to all my friends.

   a. teased   b. giggled   c. bragged   d. mourned

2. The doctor asked the family to contact her if the patient experienced anything of the slightest <u>consequence</u>.

   a. wish   b. difficulty   c. trouble   d. importance

3. I am afraid the dinner will be ruined if too many people <u>meddle</u> in its preparation.

   a. interfere   b. simmer   c. cooperate   d. triumph

4. Ben Weatherstaff said the robin was so <u>conceited</u> he would rather have stones thrown at him than not be noticed.

   a. handsome   b. aggressive   c. shy   d. vain

5. The loud noise from the apartment upstairs <u>vexes</u> me when I try to go to sleep.

   a. injures   b. irritates   c. amuses   d. rejuvenates

> Read to learn how Mary keeps busy during the rainy days.

Questions:

1. Why is Martha frightened when Mary tells her she has visited Colin?
2. Why is Colin's uncle a poor choice as a doctor for him?
3. Why does Mary think that Colin should meet Dickon?
4. Why does Mary wait some time before taking Colin to the garden?
5. Why do Mary and Dickon decide to share their garden with Colin?

Questions for Discussion:

1. Why do you think Colin seemed a different person to Mary than he was with anyone else at Misselthwaite Manor?
2. Do you think it is possible for a person to have physical symptoms of illness that reflect emotional problems? Do you think Colin's problems are mainly physical or emotional?

Chapters 14, 15 (cont.)

Literary Element: Characterization

Return to the Venn diagram you began in the last chapter unit and add additional information, particularly showing similarities between Mary and Colin and differences between Colin and Dickon.

Writing Activity:

When Mary returned to the garden after being shut in the house for many rainy days, she was thrilled to see how it changed. It was as though she were seeing it all for the first time. Describe a place that you have come back to after a period of absence. Tell how it changed or in what ways it appeared to change. Also, tell whether you preferred it before or after your absence.

CHAPTERS 16 – 19

Vocabulary: In each sentence below there is one word that does not make sense. Circle that word and write an appropriate word from the Word Box on the line below.

WORD BOX		
doleful	ferociously	unscrupulous
ecstasy	perplexed	

1. My little sister was so angry that she stamped her foot timidly and marched out of the room.

   _____

2. When told that she had not received a letter from her best friend, the girl had a happy expression on her face.

   _____

3. Only an honest man would cheat his family out of their inheritance.

   _____

4. The teacher was pleased by the student who never had to study, but could do well on all her exams.

   _____

5. An expression of boredom lit up her face when she received the puppy she had always wanted.

   _____

> Read to find out why Mary decides it is time to take Colin to the garden.

Questions:

1. Why does Colin's nurse feel that it is good for Colin to have an argument with Mary?

2. Why do all the adults in the house come to Mary for help when Colin has a tantrum?

3. How is Mary able to stop Colin's tantrums and hysterics when the nurse cannot?

4. What does Dr. Craven mean when he tells Mrs. Medlock, "It is certainly a new state of affairs . . . and there's no denying it is better than the old one"?

5. What is Colin's first impression of Dickon when they meet?

Chapters 16 – 19 (cont.)

Questions for Discussion:

1. Why do you think Mary is so insensitive to Colin's needs?

2. Do you think Mary is too tough on Colin?

3. What do you think people might have been whispering about when they observed Colin as a young child? How did Colin's perception of their remarks shape his childhood?

4. Colin thinks he will be well if he can visit the garden and befriend the animals. Many doctors recommend that their depressed patients take care of plants or a household pet. Why do you think this might improve someone's health?

5. Why do you think Mary enjoys learning and using Yorkshire dialect?

Literary Device: Personification

What is being personified in the following passage:

> He [Colin] felt as if tight strings which had held him had loosened themselves and let him go.

_____

What does this reveal about Colin's state of mind?

_____

_____

Writing Activity:

Write about a friend who has had a strong influence on your life. Describe this person and tell how you have changed as a result of your friendship.

CHAPTERS 20 – 23

Vocabulary: Draw a line from each word on the left to its definition on the right. Then use the numbered words to fill in the blanks in the sentences below.

1. descended
2. canopy
3. acquaintance
4. tactless
5. procession
6. immense
7. domestic

a. without sensitivity
b. pertaining to the home or the family
c. covering, usually of fabric, supported on poles
d. line of people moving along in a formal manner
e. came down
f. vast; huge; boundless
g. personal knowledge; friendship

. . . .

1. It is _____ to stare at people with physical handicaps.

2. The branches of the apple tree made a(n) _____ over our heads, protecting us from the sun.

3. The little boy _____ the staircase quietly so that his parents would not know he had gotten out of bed.

4. On a warm spring day, I prefer playing outdoors to doing _____ chores.

5. The farmer surveyed his _____ field where acres of wheat were growing.

6. Through your introductions, I made the _____ of many of my new neighbors.

7. A(n) _____ of trick-or-treaters marched from house to house on Halloween.

> Read to find out why the children think their garden is magical.

Questions:

1. What preparations does Colin make for his trip to the garden? Why does he want to keep it so secretive?

2. Why does Dr. Craven accept the plan to take Colin outdoors?

3. How does Colin react to the garden?

Chapters 20 – 23 (cont.)

4. What experiences does Colin have for the first time on the day he visits the garden?

5. Why doesn't Colin realize he is rude until Mary points it out to him?

Questions for Discussion:

1. What do you think is the magic of the garden?

2. Why do you think tears come to Ben Weatherstaff's eyes when he sees Colin stand straight?

3. How do you think Colin and his father will meet?

Literary Devices:

I. *Personification*—What human qualities are being given to the poppies in the following examples:

> Satiny poppies of all tints danced in the breeze by the score, gaily defying flowers which had lived in the garden for years . . .

_____

_____

What feeling does this description give you about the garden?

_____

_____

II. *Symbolism*—What do you think the roses in the garden symbolize?

_____

_____

_____

Writing Activity:

Pretend you are Ben Weatherstaff. Write a journal entry describing the changes you have seen in Mary and your feelings when you see Colin in the garden.

CHAPTERS 24 – 27

Vocabulary: Use the context to determine the meaning of the underlined word in each of the following sentences. Then compare your definition with a dictionary definition.

1. The family's <u>bounteous</u> gift made it possible for the college to build a new library.

   Your definition: _____

   Dictionary definition: _____

2. It is normal for an actor to feel <u>anxiety</u> on opening night of a show.

   Your definition: _____

   Dictionary definition: _____

3. If you exercise regularly, your muscles should not become <u>atrophied</u>.

   Your definition: _____

   Dictionary definition: _____

4. The dog's barking warned us that an <u>intruder</u> was in the house.

   Your definition: _____

   Dictionary definition: _____

5. Because of his reputation for being a <u>hypochondriac</u>, no one believed he was really sick.

   Your definition: _____

   Dictionary definition: _____

> Read to find out how Colin and his father feel about each other when they meet.

Questions:

1. Why does Colin pretend it is difficult for him to go out in his wheelchair?

2. What contribution does the wrestler Bob Haworth make to Colin's improving health?

3. What puzzled Mrs. Medlock and Dr. Craven about Colin and Mary?

4. Why is Colin pleased with Mary's idea that he has become his mother's ghost?

5. What is meant by these lines of Yorkshire wisdom:

   Where you tend a rose, my lad,
   A thistle cannot grow.

   How do these lines apply to the characters in the story?

Chapters 24 – 27 (cont.)

6. Why did Colin's father travel so long and so far?

7. What was the importance of Mr. Craven's dream in the Austrian Tyrol?

8. Is the reunion between father and son as Colin had planned?

Questions for Discussion:

1. Do you think Colin's improved health is due to magic, God, self-determination, or a combination of these factors?

2. Why do you think Colin feels so comfortable with Mrs. Sowerby from the moment they meet?

3. What explanation would you give for Mr. Craven's need to return to Misselthwaite Manor and his ability to accept his son?

Literary Elements:

I. *Characterization*—Fill in the chart below to compare the main characters at the beginning and at the end of the book. Which characters changed and which character stayed the same? Why do you think this character remained constant?

	Beginning of Book	**End of Book**
Mary		
Colin		
Dickon		
Mr. Craven		

Chapters 24 – 27 (cont.)

II. *Plot*—The plot of a work of fiction refers to the events of a story in the order they occurred. In this book, as in many stories, the events build to a climax, or turning point. Then the problems become resolved in a series of events referred to as the falling action. Fill in the plot diagram below indicating events in the rising action, the event that is the turning point, and the series of events that comprise the falling action. Finally, tell the resolution of the novel.

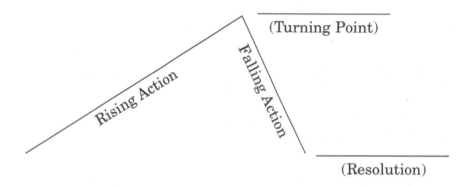

(Turning Point)

Rising Action

Falling Action

(Resolution)

III. *Setting*—The setting of a work of fiction refers to the time and place where the events of the story take place. What is the significance of the setting in *The Secret Garden*? Is time of equal importance to place in the setting of this story?

_____

_____

_____

_____

IV. *Theme*—The theme of a work of fiction refers to the author's message or the central idea of the book. What do you think are the main themes of *The Secret Garden*?

_____

_____

_____

_____

Writing Activity:

Some books have an epilogue—a chapter at the end of the book that tells about the characters' lives years after the end of the story. Create an epilogue for *The Secret Garden* in which you tell what might happen to Mary, Colin, and Dickon as adults.

CLOZE ACTIVITY

The following passage has been taken from Chapter Twenty-one of the book. Read it through entirely before replacing each blank space with a word that makes sense in context. Afterwards, you may compare your language with that of the author.

One of the strange things about living in the world is that it is only now and then one is quite sure one is going to live forever and ever and ever. One knows it sometimes when one gets _____ [1] at the tender solemn dawn-time and goes _____ [2] and stands alone and throws one's head _____ [3] back and looks up and up and _____ [4] the pale sky slowly changing and flushing _____ [5] marvelous unknown things happening until the East _____ [6] makes one cry out and one's heart _____ [7] still at the strange unchanging majesty of _____ [8] rising of the sun—which has been _____ [9] every morning for thousands and thousands and _____ [10] of years. One knows it then for _____ [11] moment or so. And one knows it _____ [12] when one stands by oneself in a _____ [13] at sunset and the mysterious deep gold _____ [14] slanting through and under the branches seems _____ [15] be saying slowly again and again something _____ [16] cannot quite hear, however much one tries. _____ [17] sometimes the immense quiet of the dark _____ [18] at night with millions of stars waiting _____ [19] watching makes one sure; and sometimes a _____ [20] of far-off music makes it true; and _____ [21] a look in some one's eyes.

And _____ [22] was like that with Colin when he _____ [23] saw and heard and felt the Springtime _____ [24] the four high walls of a hidden _____ [25]. That afternoon the whole world seemed to _____ [26] itself to being perfect and radiantly beautiful _____ [27] kind to one boy. Perhaps out of _____ [28] heavenly goodness the spring came and crowded _____ [29] it possibly could into that one place. More than once Dickon paused in what he was doing and stood still with a sort of growing wonder in his eyes, shaking his head softly.

POST-READING ACTIVITIES

1. Return to the triple Venn diagram in which you compared the characters of Mary, Colin, and Dickon on page fifteen of this study guide. Add more information and share your responses with your classmates.

2. *The Secret Garden* was first published in 1911. Why do you think it has endured for so many years as a classic for young readers? Do you think any parts of it seem old-fashioned? What parts of the book speak to today's generation of young people?

3. **Science Connection:** Imagine that you have a plot of ground to plant a garden. Research the kinds of flowers that grow well in the climate and soil type of your area. Plan the arrangement of a flower garden in which colors would be complementary and flowers would be blooming from spring to fall. If you have a plot of ground, you may plant the garden.

4. As Mary and Colin change, it becomes clear that the author is extolling certain human qualities and criticizing others. In a chart, such as the one below, make a list of the positive and negative qualities stated in the book.

Positive Qualities	Negative Qualities

5. **Pair/Share:** The author of a work of fiction tries to mold the reader's opinion of characters in the story. Work with a partner to discuss the following issues of character:

    *   Was the reader to feel sympathy for Mr. Craven despite his neglect of fatherly duties?

    *   Should the reader believe that Dr. Craven was plotting against Colin?

    *   Was the reader to forgive Mary her sour personality and Colin's arrogance at the beginning of the story?

    *   Was Dickon meant to be a believable character?

6. The book ends with the dramatic reunion of Archibald Craven and his son Colin. We can only imagine how the nurse and Dr. Craven reacted when they learned of Colin's complete recovery, or how Mary explained to her uncle all that had happened during his absence. Write an additional ending to the story from the point of view of one of these characters.

7. Imagine that ten years have passed since the end of the story and Colin and Mary are twenty years old. Write a letter as Colin or Mary might write to the other, telling about the events of the last ten years and about life now.

Post-Reading Activities (cont.)

8. **Art Connection:** Create a shoebox diorama depicting one scene in the story. It could be the garden or Colin's room at the Manor or another setting of your choice. Use actual objects, pictures taken from magazines, and scaled-down models of objects that you construct.

9. View a film version of *The Secret Garden*. Was the garden and were the characters as you expected them to be? Were any scenes left out, changed, or added? Do you think the roles of the characters were well cast? Did you prefer the book or the film?

10. **Literature Circle:** Have a literature circle discussion in which you tell your personal reactions to *A Secret Garden*. Here are some questions and sentence starters to help your literature circle begin a discussion.

    • How are you like Colin or Mary? How are you different?
    • Do you find the characters in the novel realistic? Why or why not?
    • Which character did you like the most? The least?
    • Who else would you like to read this novel? Why?
    • What questions would you like to ask the author about this novel?
    • It was not fair when . . .
    • I would have liked to see . . .
    • I wonder . . .
    • Mary learned that . . .

SUGGESTIONS FOR FURTHER READING

* Blume, Judy. *Deenie*. Delacorte.

* Byars, Betsy. *The Pinballs*. HarperCollins.

* Dickens, Charles. *Great Expectations*. Dover.

* Fleischman, Paul. *Seedfolks*. HarperTrophy.

* Garfield, James B. *Follow My Leader*. Scholastic.

* George, Jean Craighead. *Julie of the Wolves*. HarperCollins.

  Herriot, James. *All Creatures Great and Small*. St. Martin's Griffon.

* Hunt, Irene. *The Lottery Rose*. Berkley.

* Jones, Ron. *The Acorn People*. Laurel Leaf.

  Konigsburg, E.L. *Father's Arcane Daughter*. Aladdin.

* _____. *The View From Saturday*. Atheneum.

  Pearce, Phillipa. *Tom's Midnight Garden*. Greenwillow.

  Phipson, Joan. *The Watcher in the Garden*. Greenwillow.

  Ransome, Arthur. *Swallows and Amazons*. David R. Godene.

* Spinelli, Jerry. *Maniac Magee*. Little Brown.

  Spryi, Johanna. *Heidi*. Simon & Brown.

  Stratton-Porter, Gene. *Girl of the Limberlost*. Empire Books.

* Swarthout, Glenn. *Bless the Beasts and Children*. Simon & Schuster.

  Van Allsburg, Chris. *The Garden of Abdul Gasazi*. Houghton Mifflin.

Other Books by Frances Hodgson Burnett

The Land of the Blue Flower. Kessinger.

Little Lord Fauntleroy. Dover.

A Little Princess. HarperCollins.

The Lost Prince. Penguin.

Racketty Packetty House. HarperCollins.

Sara Crewe. Scholastic.

* NOVEL-TIES Study Guides are available for these titles.

ANSWER KEY

Chapter 1

Vocabulary: 1. b 2. e 3. f 4. a 5. c 6. d; 1. desolation 2. bungalow 3. veranda 4. tyrannical 5. compound 6. cholera

Questions: 1. As an unwanted child, Mary was neglected by her parents and left totally to the care of indifferent servants. She was not apprised of the impending epidemic. 2. Mary had become self-centered and tyrannical. Probably angered by her parents' neglect, she directed her ire against the servants who had to obey all her wishes. 3. While Mary slept, her parents and many of the servants died of cholera. 4. The men assumed that everyone had died or left the house. It seemed incredible that a child could have been ignored as the crises evolved in the house all around her.

Chapters 2, 3

Vocabulary: 1. d 2. f 3. a 4. b 5. e 6. c; 1. impudent 2. brougham 3. quarrel 4. stout 5. timid 6. massive

Questions: 1. Mrs. Medlock tells Mary about Misselthwaite Manor because she feels that the place is so strange and her life there will be so lonely that she doesn't want Mary to be shocked. She wants to warn Mary that her uncle will ignore her and that she will only have the company of a few servants. 2. Mary shows no emotion as Mrs. Medlock describes life at Misselthwaite Manor. Answers to the second part of the question will vary, but should include the idea that Mary is too contrary to show any real feelings, and her new life does not seem so different from her old life in India. 3. Misselthwaite Manor seems strange and lonely because it is located in a desolate place separated from other homes by a moor. The house has over one hundred rooms, most of which are unoccupied. 4. Mary and Mrs. Medlock are met at the door by servants who indicate that the uncle does not wish to see his new charge. In fact, he will leave for an extended trip the next day. Mary is escorted to her rooms and warned not to explore the house.

Chapters 4, 5

Vocabulary: 1. f 2. d 3. c 4. b 5. a 6. e; 1. servile 2. languid 3. sturdy 4. surly 5. substantial 6. ceased

Questions: 1. Unlike servants Mary knew in India, Martha is not obsequious and servile. She states her opinions about Mary's upbringing and insists that Mary learn to help herself. 2. Martha is open-minded and curious because she has never seen dark-skinned people. Mary was conditioned by her upbringing in India to consider the dark-skinned natives as an inferior race. 3. Mary identifies with the robin red-breast that was turned out of its nest. In appreciating the bird's loneliness, she recognizes her own. 4. The robin flies back to the garden and the old gardener reveals that its home is in the secret garden. 5. Spending time outdoors on the moor was changing Mary's complexion from sallow to rosy, and she was beginning to develop a healthy appetite. 6. Mary has a mutual understanding with a robin, she has come to enjoy the outdoors, she is developing a healthy appetite, and she is beginning to develop feelings of compassion. In all, she is becoming a healthier, kinder individual.

Chapters 6 – 8

Vocabulary: 1. scowl 2. muffled 3. torrent 4. coax 5. denial 6. collie 7. corridor

Questions: 1. At first Mary thought Martha was rude and common. Now she enjoys her Yorkshire speech and the stories she tells about her family. 2. Although Mary is not too interested in reading books, finding the library will give her an occupation on a lonely, rainy day. 3. When Mrs. Medlock finds Mary wandering unsupervised through the Manor, she becomes enraged. 4. Ben Weatherstaff is unable to answer Mary's questions because the garden has been locked and untended for ten years. 5. The robin leads Mary to a key that lies hidden in the dirt outside the door to the garden. 6. Mary is intrigued by the mystery surrounding the garden. Also, she would like to have a private refuge.

Chapters 9, 10

Vocabulary: 1. f   2. d   3. g   4. e   5. a   6. c   7. b;   1. spade   2. sarcastic   3. tendrils   4. trowel   5. obstinate   6. alcove   7. civil

Questions: 1. Mary becomes excited because she realizes that all the plants in the garden have not become choked and have not died: there will be flowers growing in the spring. 2. As evidence that Mary has grown healthier, she is able to skip rope, dig for hours outdoors, and her appetite has improved. Ben says she is fatter and not so sallow. 3. Mary thinks she must keep the garden a secret because if Mr. Craven found out, he would lock it up forever. 4. Mary asked Martha if the scullery-maid had a toothache because she wants to learn the source of the crying sounds she hears. 5. Ben is referring to the late Mrs. Craven and the rose bushes in the secret garden. 6. Mary knows it is Dickon because he seems to be in absolute harmony with nature as he sits with all the woodland animals around him.

Yorkshire
Dialect: 1. Martha is referring to her mother who gathered her wisdom from the experience of having twelve children. 2. Ben Weatherstaff is referring to the vain robin who fascinates Mary. 3. Ben Weatherstaff is referring to Mary and the way she looked when she first came to the manor.

Chapter 11 – 13

Vocabulary: 1. evergreen – the other words all name kinds of flowers   2. melancholy – the other words all name joyful moods   3. constellation – the other words all name kinds of terrain   4. otter – the other words all name kinds of birds   5. landlord – the other words all name kinds of servants

Questions: 1. Dickon is able to assure Mary that roses will grow in the spring when he cuts away old growth and discovers new shoots. 2. The four other people Mary likes are Martha, Martha's mother, Ben Weatherstaff, and the robin. 3. Dickon means that he would no sooner give away the secret of their garden than expose the nest of a woodland bird. 4. Mr. Craven has been convinced by Martha's mother to allow Mary the freedom to play outdoors and postpone having a governess. When Mary admits this is her own wish, Mr. Craven decides to wait before hiring a governess. 5. Mary is amazed to find another child in the house where she has been living, and one who appears so sickly. Colin is equally amazed to find a young girl in his house intruding upon his isolation. Each is surprised at the existence of the other and wonders if it is real or a dream. 6. Mr. Craven ignores Colin because he reminds him of his wife, and he is bitter about her death. He is also repulsed by his imagined, inherited hunchback condition. Mr. Craven has the servants give in to all of Colin's whims because he is the master's child and because he always seems near death. 7. Mary appeals to Colin's desire to have a secret. If the garden is made public, it will not be as intriguing. 8. Mary shows her first sign of affection when she touches Dickon's sleeve in her excitement over revealing the garden, and she strokes Colin's hand as she sings him to sleep.

Chapters 14, 15

Vocabulary: 1. c   2. d   3. a   4. d   5. b

Questions: 1. Martha is afraid she will be blamed and lose her job, which is her family's only source of income. 2. Dr. Craven would inherit the Manor if Colin became seriously ill and died. He has a vested interest in keeping Colin sick rather than making him well. 3. Mary thinks that Colin should meet Dickon because he could help Colin concentrate on life and living things rather than on death and illness. 4. Mary waits to take Colin to the garden because she wants to be certain he is a boy who can be trusted with the secret. 5. Mary and Dickon decide to share the garden with Colin because they think he will appreciate the garden and grow strong and healthy.

Chapters 16 – 19

Vocabulary: 1. timidly / ferociously   2. happy / doleful   3. honest / unscrupulous   4. pleased / perplexed   5. boredom / ecstasy

Questions: 1. Colin's nurse thinks it is good for her charge to have an argument with Mary because no one has ever dared to disagree with him before. If he is going to be in a bad temper, he may as well have something real to feel bad about. 2. All of the adults realize that Mary can be as temperamental as Colin and can therefore stand up to him. 3. Mary shocks Colin into silence and then proves to him that he does not have a lump on his back. 4. Dr. Craven is referring to the fact that his patient Colin no longer seems to need his services, even though he had a tantrum the day before. 5. Although Colin has been told all about Dickon, he is overwhelmed and delighted when he sees Dickon and his animal friends for the first time.

Chapters 20 – 23

Vocabulary: 1. e 2. c 3. g 4. a 5. d 6. f 7. b; 1. tactless 2. canopy 3. descended 4. domestic 5. immense 6. acquaintance 7. procession

Questions: 1. Colin tells the head gardener that all of the gardeners are to stop work and move away from the garden when he is taken out in his chair. Colin believes that a great part of the charm of the garden is its secret quality. 2. Dr. Craven accepts the plan to take Colin outdoors because he is too spineless to refute it and he has confidence in Dickon's reliability as a chaperone. 3. When Colin sees the garden, he is overwhelmed with joy and optimism, professing that he plans to live forever. 4. When Colin goes outdoors, he stands straight, walks a short distance, and digs in the earth for the first time. 5. Colin does not know he is being rude because he has been shut off from the world for a long time and all of the servants have been commanded to do his bidding. No one has ever corrected him or provided him with a model of polite behavior.

Chapters 24 – 27

Vocabulary: 1. bounteous – generous 2. anxiety – fear; nervousness 3. atrophied – degenerated; washed away 4. intruder – someone who comes in without permission or welcome 5. hypochondriac – someone who suffers from an imagined illness

Questions: 1. Colin pretends he cannot get out of the wheelchair because he doesn't want the doctor or the servants to know how strong and healthy he has become. He wants to surprise his father with the news. 2. Dickon asks Bob Haworth, the wrestler, for a series of muscle-building exercises that he could teach Colin to build up his strength. 3. Mrs. Medlock and Dr. Craven, unaware that Colin and Mary were getting food from Mrs. Sowerby and Dickon, could not understand how the children could eat so little and still grow healthier. 4. Colin is pleased that he may be his mother's ghost because then his father may become fond of him. If he becomes fond of him, Colin surmises, he may be able to help him have a happy life again. 5. If you replace disagreeable thoughts with agreeable ones, you will become physically healthy and emotionally sound. This has been true of Colin and Mary, but not of Colin's father. 6. Colin's father traveled to escape the memory of his deceased wife and avoid the invalid son whom he abhorred. 7. Mr. Craven dreamed that his wife was calling him back to the garden at the Manor. It served as a turning point in his life as the burden of gloom was beginning to lift. 8. Colin had planned to greet his father calmly and let his story unfold slowly. Instead, he charged into his father who had unexpectedly returned from the Continent. Their joy was not dampened by this unorthodox meeting.

NOTES: